101 THINGS® TO DO WITH
GRITS

101 THINGS® TO DO WITH
GRITS

HARRISS COTTINGHAM

Gibbs Smith

Second Edition
27 26 25 24 23   5 4 3 2 1

First Gibbs Smith edition published in 2006
Second Gibbs Smith edition published November 2023

Published by
Gibbs Smith
P.O. Box 667
Layton, Utah 84041

1.800.835.4993 orders
www.gibbs-smith.com

Cover art by Nicole LaRue and Ryan Thomann
Designed by Ryan Thomann and Renee Bond
Printed and bound in China
Gibbs Smith books are printed on either recycled, 100% post-consumer
waste, FSC-certified papers or on paper produced from sustainable PEFC-
certified forest/controlled wood source. Learn more at www.pefc.org.

The Library of Congress has cataloged the first edition as follows:

Cottingham, Harriss.
101 things to do with grits / Harriss Cottingham.—1st ed.
p. cm.
ISBN 0-941711-89-7 (first edition)
1. Cookery (Corn) 2. Grits. I. Title. II. Title: One hundred one things to do with grits.
TX809.M2C68 2006
641.6'567—dc22
2006007925

ISBN: 978-1-4236-6377-5

This book is dedicated to my grandfather, Arthur Cottingham, with whom I began my apprenticeship in the kitchen at age five. He schooled me in the art of home cooking at our Sunday meal.

I also owe a tremendous debt of gratitude to my wife, Mary, for all her help and support in the process of writing this book. A special thanks to Rion Smith for being there on those late evenings and pushing me through on the keyboard. And last, but certainly not least, cheers to all my friends and family who love spending time in my kitchen.

CONTENTS

#63–78 Side Dishes

#79–97 Desserts

#98–101 Hominy Grits

Helpful Hints

- Any flavored grits can be prepared ahead of time and stored for up to 5 days, as long as they are to be used in a cold recipe. Reheating could result in separation because of the heavy cream and butter used in most recipes.

- It is best not to reheat grits, as you are trying to maintain a smooth, creamy consistency. Once you practice the basic recipes they shouldn't take long.

- Instant grits can be substituted in any recipe to shorten preparation time. Follow the package directions.

- When preparing grits from scratch, liberal use of cream and butter, although not standard in a low-fat recipe, always makes the dish smoother.

- Always use a nonstick pot in preparation of grits recipes. My favorite brand is available at www.berndes-cookware.com.

- Always use wooden utensils in the preparation of grits recipes and in any nonstick cookware to preserve the nonstick coating.

- Always put grits pots in warm soapy water immediately after use for ease in cleanup. Do not put nonstick pots in the dishwasher.

- Fresh herbs that are not used immediately after picking or purchase can be stored for up to a week in a damp paper towel in the refrigerator.

- Fresh milk, cream, and butter should always be added toward the end of cooking time to prevent curdling.

- To avoid burning grits on the bottom of pot, maintain medium-low heat once all liquids have been reduced.

- Anson Mills organic stone-ground grits have the best flavor and consistency. I use them in any recipe that calls for stone-ground grits. Order them at www.ansonmills.com.

- Adding grits to boiling water causes them to clump. To avoid this problem, add grits to cold water and bring them to a boil. *(This hint is courtesy of my mother, Patty Honey.)*

- Clarify butter in the microwave: Place 1 stick butter at a time in a microwave-safe dish. Cover with wax paper and microwave at 100 percent power for $1\frac{1}{4}$ to $1\frac{1}{2}$ minutes until melted. Let stand, uncovered, for 2–3 minutes until the solids settle, then gently pour off the clarified liquid. Repeat to get the amount of clarified butter needed.

- To toast nuts, place shelled nuts in a single layer in a frying pan over medium-high heat. Stir or shake nuts continually until they start to turn golden, 5–7 minutes.

BASIC
GRITS

White Stone-Ground Grits

MAKES 4 SERVINGS

2 cups	chicken broth*
1 cup	white stone-ground grits
4 tablespoons	butter
1½ cups	heavy cream
	salt and pepper

In a nonstick pot, combine chicken broth and grits. Bring
to a boil and cook for 3 minutes, stirring constantly. Turn to
medium-low heat, stir in butter, and reduce liquid by half. As
liquid reduces, add heavy cream in three or four additions,
stirring occasionally. Entire process should take 45–60 minutes.
When liquid is reduced, season with salt and pepper to taste.

*This will provide the richest flavor,
but water or organic vegetable broth
can be used in its place.

Yellow Stone-Ground Grits

MAKES 4 SERVINGS

2 cups	chicken broth
1 cup	yellow stone-ground grits
4 tablespoons	butter
1½ cups	heavy cream
	salt and pepper

In a nonstick pot, combine chicken broth and grits. Bring to a boil and cook for 3 minutes, stirring constantly. Turn to medium-low heat, stir in butter, and reduce liquid by half. As liquid reduces, add heavy cream in three or four additions, stirring occasionally. Entire process should take 45–60 minutes. When liquid is reduced, season with salt and pepper to taste.

Instant Grits Done Right

MAKES 4–6 SERVINGS

2 cups	chicken or vegetable broth
1 cup	uncooked instant grits
1 stick	butter
2 teaspoons	kosher salt
2 teaspoons	black pepper
3 dashes	Tabasco sauce

Place broth in a nonstick pot and add grits. Cook grits according to package directions. Add butter, salt, pepper, and Tabasco sauce. Mix and serve.

FLAVORED GRITS

Truffle-Scented Grits

MAKES 4 SERVINGS

1 tablespoon	butter
1 cup	finely chopped portobello mushrooms
2 teaspoons	white truffle oil
	White Stone-Ground Grits (see page 12)

In a frying pan, brown butter and sauté mushrooms over high heat for 2–3 minutes or until soft. Stir together oil, sautéed mushrooms, and grits.

Savory Grits

MAKES 4 SERVINGS

¼ cup **packed fresh, aromatic
thyme leaves (no stems)
White Stone-Ground Grits
(see page 12)**

Wash and scrape the thyme leaves with a sharp knife to bruise them (this releases their oils). Add to cooked grits to enhance the flavor and complement a wide variety of dishes.

Variation: Substitute thyme with rosemary, parsley, oregano, or a mixture of these herbs, but never more than ¼ cup to one 4-serving basic recipe.

Roasted Garlic–Infused Grits

MAKES 4 SERVINGS

½ cup	whole garlic cloves
1 cup	olive oil
	White Stone-Ground Grits (see page 12)

Preheat oven to 400 degrees.

Place garlic and oil in small oven-safe ramekin and cover with foil. Bake for 45 minutes or until cloves are golden brown and softened. Strain and reserve oil.

With a fork, mash cloves into warm cooked grits. Stir in ¼ cup (or to taste) of reserved garlic-infused oil.

Chipotle Grits

MAKES 4 SERVINGS

1 can (7.5 ounces)	chipotle peppers
1 can (4.5 ounces)	chopped green chiles
1 tablespoon	apple cider vinegar
1 tablespoon	cocoa powder
pinch	kosher salt
	Yellow Stone-Ground Grits (see page 13)

In a blender or food processor, blend all ingredients except grits until smooth. While grits are hot, stir in chipotle mixture.

Red Curry Grits

MAKES 4 SERVINGS

2 tablespoons	**red curry paste**
1 can (12 ounces)	**coconut milk**
6	**basil leaves, finely chopped**
	juice of 1 lime
2	**stalks lemongrass**
	White Stone-Ground Grits (see page 12)

In a bowl, combine curry paste and coconut milk with a whisk. Add basil leaves, lime juice, and lemongrass and heat over medium-high heat for 10 minutes.

Remove lemongrass and fold cooked grits into mixture. Reduce heat to medium-low and let coconut mixture absorb into grits.

Old Bay–Lemon Grits

MAKES 4 SERVINGS

	White or Yellow Stone-Ground Grits (see pages 12 and 13)
	zest of 1 large lemon
	juice of 1 lemon
2 tablespoons	**Old Bay Seasoning**
2 tablespoons	**Tabasco sauce**
	kosher salt and pepper

After grits have cooked for just a few minutes and before adding the cream, add the lemon zest, lemon juice, and Old Bay. Continue recipe as directed. When liquid has reduced, add Tabasco sauce and salt and pepper to taste.

Gouda Grits

MAKES 4 SERVINGS

	White Stone-Ground Grits (see page 12)
1 cup	**grated Gouda cheese**
1 tablespoon	**Tabasco sauce**
	pinch white pepper

When grits are nearly ready, add cheese, Tabasco sauce, and pepper. Stir, serve and enjoy.

Variation: Substitute smoked Gouda for the Gouda to get a little different flavor.

#11

White Cheddar Cheese Grits

MAKES 4 SERVINGS

	White Stone-Ground Grits (see page 12)
1 cup	**finely grated Vermont white cheddar cheese (sharp, if you like)**
1 tablespoon	**Tabasco sauce**
	pinch white pepper

When grits are nearly ready, stir in cheese, Tabasco sauce, and pepper.

Stilton Blue Cheese Grits

MAKES 4 SERVINGS

**White Stone-Ground Grits
(see page 12)**
½ **cup** **crumbled Stilton blue cheese**
1 **tablespoon** **Worcestershire sauce**
pinch black pepper
New York strip steak

When grits are nearly ready, stir in cheese, Worcestershire sauce, and pepper. Serve with a rare New York strip steak.

#13

Espresso Grits

MAKES 4–6 SERVINGS

**White Stone-Ground Grits (see
page 12) or instant grits**
½ **cup** **cold espresso or very
strong coffee**
⅓ **cup** **dark rum**

Prepare grits and then add espresso and rum. Let grits absorb liquid.

Pesto-Flavored Grits

MAKES 4 SERVINGS

4 cups	tightly packed basil leaves, washed and stemmed
	juice of 1 lemon
1½ cups	olive oil, divided
5 cloves	garlic, finely chopped
1 cup	toasted pine nuts
2	anchovy fillets
1 cup	grated Parmigiano-Reggiano
	kosher salt and pepper
	White Stone-Ground Grits (see page 12)

In a blender or food processor, blend together basil, lemon juice, and ½ cup olive oil. While blending, add garlic, pine nuts, anchovies, and cheese. Slowly add remaining 1 cup olive oil to emulsify, and then salt and pepper to taste.

Stir ½ cup of the pesto mixture at a time into warm grits, depending on personal taste and desired strength.

Sweet Vanilla Grits

MAKES 4 SERVINGS

2 cups	**sugar water (1½ cups sugar to 2 cups water)**
1 cup	**white stone-ground grits**
2 cups	**heavy cream**
1 whole	**vanilla bean**
4 tablespoons	**vanilla extract**
2 tablespoons	**butter**

In a saucepan, combine sugar water and uncooked grits and bring to a boil. Reduce heat to low and cook for 45–60 minutes.

In a separate saucepan, slowly simmer cream over medium heat. Slice vanilla bean down center and scrape seeds from husk, adding them to cream with vanilla bean stalk. Add vanilla extract and simmer for 30–45 minutes until cream becomes aromatic; reduce by one-fourth. Discard the bean and then add mixture and butter to grits and stir.

Chocolate Grits

MAKES 4 SERVINGS

2 cups	sugar water (1½ cups sugar to 2 cups water)
1 cup	white stone-ground grits*
4 tablespoons	vanilla extract
2 cups	heavy cream, divided
½ cup	cocoa powder
4 tablespoons	butter
½ pound	Ghirardelli milk chocolate, sliced into slivers

In a saucepan, combine sugar water, uncooked grits, and vanilla extract. Bring to boil and reduce heat to low. Add 1 cup cream and cocoa powder to grits. Add additional cocoa, if necessary, to achieve rich, dark color. Add remaining 1 cup cream, butter, and chocolate. Stir and cook on medium low for about 45 minutes until liquid is absorbed.

*For a smoother texture, use instant grits. The cooking time will be 10–15 minutes.

Pistachio Grits

MAKES 4 SERVINGS

2 cups	sugar water (1½ cups sugar to 2 cups water)
1 cup	white stone-ground grits
4 tablespoons	vanilla extract
½ cup	shelled toasted pistachio nuts, ground fine in a food processor
4 tablespoons	butter
4 tablespoons	pistachio syrup or extract
2 cups	heavy cream

In a saucepan, bring sugar water and uncooked grits to boil. Reduce heat to low. Add vanilla, nuts, butter, and pistachio syrup. As grits absorb liquid, add cream in two additions, stirring occasionally. Cook 45 minutes on low or until liquid is absorbed.

Hazelnut Grits

MAKES 4 SERVINGS

½ cup	shelled toasted hazelnuts
2 cups	sugar water (1½ cups sugar to 2 cups water)
1 cup	white stone-ground grits
4 tablespoons	vanilla extract
4 tablespoons	butter
4 tablespoons	hazelnut syrup or extract
2 cups	heavy cream

While hot, place toasted hazelnuts in a kitchen dish towel and roll together to remove bitter outer skin. Grind finely in a food processor and set aside.

In a saucepan, combine sugar water and uncooked grits. Bring to a boil and reduce heat to low. Add vanilla, nuts, butter, and hazelnut syrup. As grits absorb liquid, add cream in two additions, stirring occasionally until liquid is absorbed, about 45 minutes.

Strawberry Grits

MAKES 4–6 SERVINGS

1 cup	instant grits
1 teaspoon	strawberry extract
2 tablespoons	unsalted butter
1 cup	chopped fresh strawberries
½ cup	granulated sugar

Prepare grits according to package directions and add extract.

In a frying pan, heat butter over medium-high heat, and once foam dissipates, add strawberries and sugar. Cook for 4–6 minutes, or until sugar has melted into a nice amount of strawberry syrup. Set aside to cool. Once grits have cooled, puree strawberries and syrup in a blender and fold into grits.

Key Lime Grits
MAKES 4–6 SERVINGS

1 cup	water
1 cup	Key lime juice
1 cup	instant grits
4 tablespoons	vanilla extract
2 cups	heavy cream
1 whole	vanilla bean
2 tablespoons	butter

In a pot, combine water, lime juice and grits. Bring to a boil and reduce heat to low. Cook for 15 minutes or until liquid is absorbed.

In a separate pot, add vanilla extract and cream. Bring to a slow simmer over medium heat. Slice vanilla bean down center and scrape seeds from husk into cream, adding vanilla bean stalk. Simmer for 30–45 minutes until cream becomes aromatic; reduce by one-fourth. Discard vanilla bean. Add mixture to grits and stir in butter.

BREAKFAST

Shrimp and Grits with Bacon and Cheddar

MAKES 4 SERVINGS

2 cups	Yellow or White Stone-Ground Grits (see pages 12 and 13)
1 pound	Carolina Pride thick-cut bacon
1	large sweet onion, diced
4 cloves	garlic, diced
1 pound (26–30)	shrimp, peeled (local fresh shrimp, when in season)
⅓ cup	Worcestershire sauce
¼ cup	white wine
	Tabasco sauce
2 cups	grated extra-sharp cheddar cheese

Pour cooked grits into 9 x 13-inch pan. Preheat oven to 350 degrees.

Cook bacon until crisp in a nonstick frying pan. Turn out onto paper towels and drain, reserving bacon grease in pan. Heat frying pan to medium high. Caramelize onion and garlic in reserved bacon grease until brown. Add shrimp and cook 3–5 minutes. Combine Worcestershire and wine and deglaze pan with liquid, stirring frequently. Reduce liquid by half or until slightly thickened. Remove from heat. Pour shrimp-and-onion mixture over grits. Season to taste with Tabasco sauce. Top with cheese, and then bake 15–20 minutes or until cheese is bubbly and melted.

Veggie Omelets
MAKES 6–8 SERVINGS

1 dozen	large eggs
	kosher salt and pepper
2 dashes	Tabasco sauce
2 stems	fresh rosemary, chopped
3 stems	fresh thyme, chopped
3/4 cup	heavy cream
1/4 cup	butter, cut into tablespoons
1	red onion, diced
1 bunch	asparagus
1/2 cup	sliced fresh mushrooms
1	red pepper, julienned
1	green pepper, julienned
	White Cheddar Cheese Grits (see page 23)
1 cup	grated white cheddar cheese

In a large bowl, mix eggs, salt and pepper, Tabasco sauce, rosemary, thyme, and heavy cream. Mix well, about 6 minutes. Preheat a frying pan to high heat, add 1 tablespoon of butter, and sauté onion until brown. Break asparagus in half. Add asparagus, mushrooms, and red and green peppers to onion and cook until just tender. Divide veggies into six to eight equal portions.

Heat a nonstick frying pan to medium high and place 1 tablespoon of butter in the pan. Ladle out about 4 ounces egg mixture into pan. Using a rubber spatula, scrape edges of pan, allowing eggs to cook. Once most of the eggs are cooked, add a layer of grits on half of the omelet, top with one portion veggies and fold over, browning each side of the omelet. Garnish with cheese, and repeat to make remaining omelets.

Old-Fashioned Salmon and Grits

MAKES 6–8 SERVINGS

1½ cans (14.5 ounces each)	pink salmon, liquid reserved
2	eggs
1 tablespoon	olive oil
¼ cup	chopped onion
¼ cup	chopped scallions
¼ cup	chopped green bell pepper
	salt and pepper
1 cup	grated sharp cheddar cheese
	White Stone-Ground Grits (see page 12)

Preheat oven to 350 degrees.

Break up salmon and drain, reserving ½ cup of liquid. Combine eggs and salmon liquid and set aside. Preheat medium frying pan over medium-high heat. Add the olive oil, onions, and bell pepper, sautéing until onions and peppers are brown. Add salt and pepper to taste. Pour half the cooked grits into the bottom of a 9 x 13-inch greased pan. Then layer half the salmon, onion mixture, and cheese. Add remaining grits, then remaining salmon mixture, adding the remaining cheese and onion mixture last. Pour the egg mixture over top and bake 25–30 minutes.

Salmon and Grits Terrine
MAKES 6–8 SERVINGS

1 pound	fresh salmon fillet
3 sprigs	fresh dill
3 stems	fresh tarragon
3 stems	fresh thyme
5 tablespoons	butter, divided
2 bunches	scallions, chopped
	White Stone-Ground Grits (see page 12)

Preheat oven to 400 degrees. Bake salmon 12–16 minutes, or until fish flakes to the touch. Let salmon cool and then break into small pieces in a bowl. Chop all herbs finely, discarding any woody stems, and mix with salmon. Pour 4 tablespoons melted butter over salmon-and-herb mixture. Sauté scallions in remaining 1 tablespoon of butter until browned.

Line a loaf pan with parchment paper, getting it as smooth as possible. Pour small amount of cooked grits into loaf pan, and then top with salmon mixture and scallions. Repeat layering until all ingredients have been used. Cover with parchment paper and refrigerate for 4 hours to set. Remove from refrigerator and unmold. Cut into 3/4-inch slices and serve.

Eggs Benedict

MAKES 12 SERVINGS

Hollandaise sauce:

1 pound	clarified unsalted butter
6	egg yolks
$\frac{1}{4}$ cup	white wine
2 tablespoons	white vinegar
2 dashes	Tabasco sauce
	juice of 1 lemon
	white pepper and kosher salt
1 cup	water

	poaching liquid (3 quarts water, $\frac{1}{2}$ cup white vinegar, 1 tablespoon kosher salt)
$\frac{1}{2}$ pound	Canadian bacon, sliced
1 package	English muffins
1 dozen	eggs
	White or Yellow Stone-Ground Grits (see pages 12 and 13)

Preheat oven to 400 degrees. In a saucepan, melt butter and then keep it warm. Whisk yolks in a stainless steel bowl. Add wine, vinegar, Tabasco, lemon juice, and pepper and salt. Mix to incorporate all ingredients.

In a 2-quart saucepan or double boiler, bring the water to a soft boil. Place bowl with egg mixture on top. Whisk yolk mixture for 3–5 minutes. Do not stop; the yolks expand by whisking air into them. Avoid overcooking yolks. Once mixture has a glossy look and is thick, remove from heat and slowly add melted butter in three additions, whisking constantly to incorporate. Keep sauce warm, but off direct heat.

Heat poaching liquid to 180 degrees or when small bubbles form on bottom of pan. Place Canadian bacon on a baking sheet and bake 15 minutes. Toast muffins and poach eggs for 3–5 minutes, depending on desired doneness. Place half a muffin on a plate. Top with grits, Canadian bacon, egg, and Hollandaise sauce.

#26
Sweet Porridge with Fresh Fruit

MAKES 4–6 SERVINGS

	fresh fruit (blackberries, raspberries, strawberries, or any fruit you like)
	Sweet Vanilla Grits (see page 26)
¼ cup	heavy cream, cold
½ cup	packed brown sugar

Wash and slice fruit, as needed. In a small bowl, add a portion of grits and top with fruit, cream, and brown sugar.

Country Ham and Redeye Gravy

MAKES 6–8 SERVINGS

¹⁄₄ cup	unsalted butter
¹⁄₂ pound	country-style ham
¹⁄₂ cup	coffee
¹⁄₄ cup	boiling water
2–3 dashes	Cholula hot sauce
	White Stone-Ground Grits (see page 12)

Preheat a large cast-iron frying pan to medium-high heat. Melt butter and fry ham on each side for 2–3 minutes, turning ham only once, and then place on a serving platter. Deglaze frying pan with a mixture of coffee and boiling water, making sure to scrape the pan for all drippings. Cook for 3–5 minutes to boiling, or when mixture reduces by one-fourth. Remove from heat and add hot sauce. Serve cooked grits with a small indentation in the top for gravy accompanied by ham.

Biscuits with Sausage and Grits Gravy

MAKES 4–6 SERVINGS

1 pound	spicy sausage
1 bag	frozen buttermilk biscuits
2 packages	sausage gravy mix
	White Stone-Ground Grits (see page 12)
1 pinch	kosher salt
2 tablespoons	coarse ground black pepper
4–6	eggs

In a frying pan over medium-high heat, crumble sausage and cook until browned. Bake the biscuits according to package directions and set aside. Prepare gravy according to package directions and mix with sausage. Stir gravy into cooked grits until incorporated. Serve over biscuits with eggs cooked to order. Season with salt and pepper.

Corned Beef Grits Hash

MAKES 4–6 SERVINGS

1	Spanish onion, diced
2 cloves	garlic, minced
¼ cup	butter, divided
2 cups	diced cooked corned beef
2 tablespoons	stone-ground mustard
scant pinch	ground nutmeg
1 tablespoon	dried Italian spices
	White Stone-Ground Grits (see page 12)
8–12	eggs
4–6 pieces	toast

In a frying pan over medium-high heat, cook onions and garlic in 2 tablespoons butter until browned , 8–10 minutes. Add corned beef, mustard, and spices. Cook for 2–3 minutes so ingredients incorporate well. In a bowl, mix together cooked grits and beef mixture. Refrigerate at least 3 hours.

Preheat a large cast-iron frying pan to medium-high heat, add remaining 2 tablespoons butter to coat, and press hash mixture into pan, molding mixture to form of pan. Shake pan to prevent sticking. Brown hash on each side. Remove from heat. Place a plate on top of pan and flip hash onto plate. Serve with eggs and toast.

Chipotle Omelets
MAKES 4–6 SERVINGS

1 dozen	eggs
	salt and pepper
3 dashes	Tabasco sauce
	chopped sage
¾ cup	heavy cream
¼ cup	butter, cut into tablespoons
	Chipotle Grits (see page 19)
1 jar (12 ounces)	roasted red peppers, sliced
1 can (7.5 ounces)	chipotle peppers, sliced
1 cup	grated spicy jack cheese
	hash browns
	fresh fruit

In a large bowl, mix eggs with salt and pepper, Tabasco sauce, sage, and cream. Mix well, about 6 minutes.

Heat a nonstick frying pan to medium-high heat and place 1 tablespoon butter in the pan. Ladle in about 6 ounces of egg mixture. Using a rubber spatula, scrape edges of pan, allowing eggs to cook. Once most of the eggs are cooked, add a layer of grits on half the omelet. Place a portion of red and chipotle peppers and then cheese on top of grits, fold over and brown on both sides, and repeat to make remaining omelets. Serve with hash browns and fresh fruit.

Tomato-Basil Quiche

MAKES 6 SERVINGS

1 dozen	eggs
1½ cups	heavy cream
	salt and pepper
2 ounces	basil, washed and cut fine
1 pint (8 ounces)	cherry tomatoes, halved
¼ cup	balsamic vinegar
2	deep-dish pie shells
1 cup	crumbled tomato basil feta cheese
	White Stone-Ground Grits (see page 12)

Preheat oven to 375 degrees.

In a bowl, mix eggs, cream, and salt and pepper to taste. In a separate bowl, mix basil, tomatoes, and vinegar and toss with salt and pepper to taste. Divide vegetable mixture between two pie shells and then top with feta. Mix half the grits with eggs and pour mixture into pie shells, dividing between the two. Bake on middle rack for 30 minutes. Rotate quiche a full turn and bake another 15 minutes or until firm and browned on top.

APPETIZERS

Stuffed Mushrooms

MAKES 6–8 SERVINGS

2 pounds	baby portobello mushrooms, stemmed
	Truffle-Scented Grits (see page 16)
1 log	pepper-encrusted goat cheese, crumbled

Preheat oven to 350 degrees.

Clean mushrooms with fine brush to remove dirt, or lightly wash without allowing them to absorb water. Fill each mushroom cap with a spoonful of grits and then top with goat cheese. Arrange each cap on a baking sheet. Bake for 30–45 minutes, or until mushrooms are soft to touch.

Hot Cajun Crab Dip

MAKES 4–6 SERVINGS

1 can (8 ounces)	lump blue crabmeat
1 can (8 ounces)	crab claw meat
	Old Bay–Lemon Grits (see page 21)
1 cup	grated sharp cheddar cheese
1 tablespoon	Old Bay Seasoning
	crackers of choice

Preheat oven to 350 degrees.

In a bowl, mix together crabmeat and crab claw meat. Fold into cooked grits. Place in an 8 x 8-inch oven-safe baking dish and sprinkle with cheese. Bake for 45 minutes. Remove from oven and garnish with Old Bay Seasoning. Serve with your favorite crackers.

Roasted Garlic and Chive Terrine

MAKES 6–8 SERVINGS

1 bunch	thin asparagus
	Roasted Garlic–Infused Grits (see page 18)
2 bunches	chives, chopped
1 jar (12 ounces)	roasted red peppers

Trim and blanch asparagus. Layer grits, chives, asparagus, and red peppers in a loaf pan lined with plastic wrap. Repeat until pan is full. Press ingredients into mold. Cover and chill for 4–6 hours. Remove from mold and cut into $\frac{1}{4}$-inch slices.

#35
Spinach and Artichoke Dip
MAKES 4–6 SERVINGS

	juice of 1 lemon
½ cup	mayonnaise
1½ cups	Parmesan cheese
¼ cup	sour cream
1½ cans (14.5 ounces each)	artichokes, drained and diced
1 package (8 ounces)	frozen spinach, thawed and drained
	Roasted Garlic–Infused Grits (see page 18)
	pita chips

Preheat oven 400 degrees.

In a bowl, add all ingredients to cooked grits and mix well. Place in an 8 x 8-inch oven-safe baking dish and bake for 45 minutes. Serve hot with pita chips.

#36

Grits Maki

MAKES 6-8 SERVINGS

4 bunches	collard greens
2	Granny Smith apples, peeled and cut into small pieces
6 pack	Heineken beer
	kosher salt and pepper
12 ounces	pickled ginger
1 jar (2 ounces)	wasabi powder
1 pound	boiled shrimp (use an Old Bay Seasoning bag in your water)
	White Stone-Ground Grits (see page 12)
2	cucumbers, peeled, seeded and cut into long thin strips
4	Roma tomatoes, seeded and julienned
	soy sauce

Cut ribs out of collards. Discard ribs and mix greens with apples. Place mixture into a stockpot and add five beers (you can drink the remaining one!) with two pinches kosher salt, half the pickled ginger, and all the ginger juice. Bring collards to a boil and boil for 5 minutes. Reduce heat to medium-low, and cook for 1 hour, or until tender. Let cool.

Make wasabi paste by following directions on wasabi powder jar. Stir 1½ tablespoons paste into cooked grits.

Peel shrimp; slice in half lengthwise. Place greens one piece at a time onto cutting board and overlap until there is a 2 x 6-inch sheet of greens. Place a layer of wasabi grits on collards and spread evenly. Place four strips of cucumbers, six strips of tomato, and six pieces of shrimp down middle of roll. Place small amount of mixed wasabi paste on the outside edge of the roll. Roll outside edge into middle and finish by rolling through; make sure to roll it tight. Chill roll for 1 hour; cut into six to eight pieces. Serve with remaining 6 ounces ginger, wasabi, and soy sauce.

Recipe courtesy of Executive Chef Craig Fincher.

#37
Salmon and Grits Cakes
MAKES 4–6 SERVINGS

	Old Bay–Lemon Grits (see page 21)
2 pounds	**smoked salmon**
1½ cups	**House-Autry Seafood Breader**
2 tablespoons	**butter**
2 tablespoons	**vegetable oil**
1 container (8 ounces)	**sour cream**
1 large	**red onion, diced fine chives, for garnish**

Let grits cool to room temperature. Break up salmon and add to grits. Pat grit mixture into six to eight small pancake-like patties. Coat patties with seafood breader and pan sauté in butter and oil until crisp and golden brown. Serve with a dollop of sour cream, diced onion, and a few chives.

Fried Shrimp-and-Grits Balls

MAKES 4–6 SERVINGS

8 ounces	peeled tiger shrimp, washed and chopped into small pieces
3 tablespoons	butter
	kosher salt and pepper
6 ounces	pickled jalapeño peppers
	White Stone-Ground Grits (see page 12)
5 cups	vegetable oil
	House-Autry Seafood Breader
	cocktail sauce

Sauté shrimp in a hot pan with butter and salt and pepper until firm. Stir shrimp and jalapeños into the cooked grits. Pour shrimp-and-grit mixture onto a sheet pan and let cool to room temperature; place in refrigerator for 4–6 hours.

Bring oil to 375 degrees in a frying pot or deep fryer. Make ½-inch balls out of the cold grits, coat evenly with seafood breader, and fry five to eight balls at a time, depending on how big the fryer is, until golden brown with a crispy outside.

Serve with cocktail sauce or use as a side item with an entrée. They go great with low-country red rice and good southern coleslaw.

Velveeta Mexican Dip
MAKES 4–6 SERVINGS

1 pound	**Velveeta Mexican cheese**
1 can (8 ounces)	**Rotel tomatoes, drained**
1 can (4.5 ounces)	**green chiles**
¼ cup	**salsa**
	Yellow Stone-Ground Grits (see page 13)
1 bag	**tortilla chips**

Microwave cheese in a microwave-safe bowl, and mix well with tomatoes, chiles, and salsa. Add mixture to cooked grits in two additions, mixing well each time. Serve hot with tortilla chips.

Variation: Add 1 jar (12 ounces) roasted red peppers, diced.

Southwestern Seven-Layer Dip

MAKES 8–10 SERVINGS

	Chipotle Grits (see page 19)
2 cans (8 ounces each)	refried beans
16 ounces	sour cream
16 ounces	guacamole dip
1 jar (8 ounces)	salsa
1 cup	grated sharp cheddar cheese
1 cup	grated pepper jack cheese
1 jar (8 ounces)	pickled jalapeños
1 small can (4.5 ounces)	black olives, sliced
3 cans (4 ounces each)	diced green chiles

Layer ingredients in order as listed above on a round platter and chill for 2 hours. Serve with chips, lime, and cold beer.

Sausage Dip

MAKES 4–6 SERVINGS

1 package (8 ounces)	cream cheese, at room temperature
1 can (8 ounces)	Rotel tomatoes, drained
	White Stone-Ground Grits (see page 12)
1 pound	spicy sausage
2 tablespoons	butter
1 teaspoon	ground thyme
1 teaspoon	ground sage
	crackers, corn chips, or toast points

Add cream cheese and tomatoes to hot grits. In a large nonstick sauté pan over medium-high heat, cook sausage with butter until browned, 6–8 minutes; add thyme and sage. When cooked through, stir together with grits. Serve with choice of crackers, corn chips, or toast points.

Pesto Toast Points with Beef Tenderloin

MAKES ABOUT 20 SERVINGS

	juice of 2 lemons
2 tablespoons	white vinegar
½ cup	olive oil, divided
1 tablespoon	Worcestershire sauce
1 pound	high-quality beef tenderloin, center cut and trimmed
	fresh-cracked coarse black pepper
	kosher salt
1	French baguette, sliced ¼ inch thick
3 tablespoons each	chopped fresh thyme, parsley and rosemary
	Pesto-Flavored Grits (see page 25)
¼ cup	grated Parmigiano-Reggiano

Combine lemon juice, vinegar, ¼ cup oil, and Worcestershire sauce in a plastic ziplock bag with beef. Refrigerate for at least 2 hours. Remove beef from bag and generously coat with salt and pepper. Sear beef over high heat on all sides, about 1 minute per side or 3–5 minutes total. Place in freezer for 2 hours.

Preheat oven to 350 degrees. Place baguette slices in a large mixing bowl and coat with remaining ¼ cup olive oil, herbs, and a pinch of salt and pepper. Bake on a baking sheet for 12–15 minutes, or until golden brown.

Remove beef from freezer and slice thin. Place slices between two layers of plastic wrap. Pat lightly with a medium serving spoon until meat becomes very thin. Spoon pesto grits onto toast. Top with beef and garnish with cheese.

ENTRÉES

Roasted Pork Loin with Apple Compote

MAKES 4–6 SERVINGS

2 tablespoons	butter
3	large tart apples, peeled and sliced into small pieces
¼ cup	brown sugar
1 small log	goat cheese
2 pounds	pork tenderloin or pork roast kosher salt and pepper
1 teaspoon	garlic powder
1 teaspoon	cumin
1 teaspoon	onion powder
	Chipotle Grits (see page 19)

Preheat oven to 400 degrees.

Heat a frying pan to high heat, add butter, let foam stop, and then add apples and brown sugar, cooking until apples are soft, 8–10 minutes. Add goat cheese, reduce to medium heat, and mix until well incorporated. Set aside. Place pork on a clean work surface and coat with salt and pepper, garlic powder, cumin, and onion powder. Braise all sides of pork in a hot pan to lock in flavor. Cook pork in oven until cooked through, or until it reaches an internal temperature of 145–160 degrees. Time will vary depending on the cut. Let pork rest for 10 minutes before slicing. Place grits in a serving dish and place sliced pork over the grits. Top with apple compote.

#44
Old-Timey White Grits with Meatballs

MAKES 4–6 SERVINGS

	White Stone-Ground Grits (see page 12) or instant grits
2 pounds	**ground beef**
	kosher salt and pepper
1 teaspoon	**garlic powder**
½ cup	**Worcestershire sauce, divided**
2½ tablespoons	**butter**
¼ cup	**coffee**

If using instant grits, follow package directions.

In a bowl, combine beef, salt and pepper, garlic powder, and 2 tablespoons Worcestershire sauce. Make meatballs to desired size.

In a frying pan, heat butter over medium-high heat and cook meatballs until they have an internal temperature of 160 degrees, 12–15 minutes, depending on size. Large meatballs may require a few minutes in oven at 350 degrees to finish cooking through. Arrange meatballs over cooked grits. Deglaze pan with remaining 6 tablespoons Worcestershire and coffee. Cook and scrape down sides, reduce by one-fourth, and spoon over meatballs.

Seafood Paella

MAKES 4–6 SERVINGS

½ cup	heavy cream
½ cup	white wine
2 big pinches	saffron
	kosher salt and pepper
6 ounces	clams
6 ounces	green lip mussels
½ pound	shrimp, peeled
6 ounces	medium scallops
1 large	onion, diced
1 pound	spicy link sausage
	White Stone-Ground Grits (see page 12)
	hot sauce

In a pot, bring cream and wine to simmer; add saffron, and salt and pepper. Place all seafood in cream mixture and cook until shrimp float, about 5 minutes.

In a frying pan, brown onion, add sausage, and cook through, 6–8 minutes. Add seafood mixture to onions and reduce by half. Stir mixture into grits and serve with hot sauce to taste.

#46
Shrimp and Scallop Scampi
MAKES 4–6 SERVINGS

3 tablespoons	unsalted butter
½ pound	medium scallops, patted dry
2 tablespoons	vegetable oil
1 pound	medium shrimp, peeled (fresh if in season)
2 large	shallots, minced
2 cloves	garlic, minced
2 tablespoons	finely chopped parsley
2 sprigs	fresh thyme, steamed and chopped
	juice of 1 lemon
⅓ cup	sauvignon blanc
	Savory Grits (see page 17)

Heat a large frying pan to medium high and then add butter and scallops. Brown both sides of the scallops, about 3 minutes per side, remove from pan, and set aside.

Add oil to the same frying pan and heat over medium high. Add shrimp and cook for 4 minutes, then add shallots, garlic, parsley, and thyme. Cook for 4 more minutes, then add lemon juice and wine.

Add the scallops to the shrimp mixture and sauté for about 3 minutes more, or until scallops are firm on the outside and liquid has reduced and thickened. Serve over grits while hot.

Pan-Fried Lobster Tails

MAKES 4–6 SERVINGS

3 large	lobster tails
1 cup	House-Autry Seafood Breader
¼ cup	butter
	Old Bay–Lemon Grits (see page 21)
1 can (16 ounces)	lobster claw meat
5 stems	fresh lemon thyme, chopped

Remove lobster meat from shell and lightly bread with seafood breader.

In a frying pan, melt butter on high heat, add lobster tails, and fry until golden brown, 8–11 minutes depending on the size. Arrange over grits. Toss claw meat in drippings to warm. Spoon drippings and meat over lobster tails. Garnish with fresh thyme.

Yellow Stone-Ground Grits with Southern Caviar

MAKES 4–6 SERVINGS

1 can (8 ounces)	white corn
1 can (8 ounces)	black-eyed peas
1 jar	roasted red peppers
2 cloves	garlic, minced
½	red onion, diced fine
1 tablespoon	whole-grain mustard
2 tablespoons	white vinegar
6 ounces	spicy relish
	Yellow Stone-Ground Grits (see page 13)

Drain corn and black-eyed peas in a fine mesh strainer, rinse, and set aside. Chop peppers into small pieces and combine with corn-and-pea mixture, garlic, onion, mustard, vinegar, and relish in a large bowl. Mix well and chill for at least 1 hour. After the Southern caviar has chilled, cook grits and serve the caviar over top hot grits.

Farm-Raised Quail with Mushroom Gravy

MAKES 6 SERVINGS

2 cups	uncooked grits (your choice)
	kosher salt and pepper
4 tablespoons	Lawry's Poultry Seasoning
6	fresh quail, washed and dried (or substitute Cornish game hens or chicken breasts)
6 small	sprigs fresh rosemary
1 stick	unsalted butter, room temperature and cut into small pieces
12 ounces	fresh mushrooms, cleaned and quartered
1 cup	Marsala cooking wine

Prepare grits according to directions. Preheat oven to 400 degrees.

In a small bowl, mix 4 pinches kosher salt and 4 pinches pepper with poultry seasoning. Coat the quail evenly with this mixture. Put the rosemary inside the cavity of the birds. Bake 1 hour, or until internal temperature reaches 165–175 degrees. Remove from oven and let rest 10 minutes. While oven cools, cover and then place quail back in warm oven.

Heat a large frying pan over medium-high heat and add 2 tablespoons butter, let foam dissipate, and add mushrooms, sautéing until aromatic and browned. Deglaze pan with wine and bring to a boil, reducing by one-fourth. Remove from heat and add remaining butter a few pieces at a time, letting most of it melt before adding more. Do not put pan back on heat after adding butter because the butter and wine will separate. Serve quail with grits topped with mushroom gravy.

Hickory-Smoked Chicken

MAKES 6 SERVINGS

1 bag	hickory/mesquite wood chips (at the grocery store in the charcoal aisle)
1	chicken, cut into legs, thighs, breasts, and wings
1 container (2.75 ounces)	McCormick Grill Mates Montreal Chicken Seasoning
1 pinch	kosher salt
1 pinch	pepper
	Pesto-Flavored Grits (see page 25)

Soak 4 cups wood chips in water for at least 1 hour. Season chicken generously with chicken seasoning, salt, and pepper. Light some charcoal for the grill. Once charcoal is ready, keep coals to one side. Place 2 cups drained wood chips on the coals and then cook chicken indirectly by placing on grill on the opposite side from the coals. Cover and let smoke for 30 minutes, then remove lid and flip chicken. Add 1 more cup wood chips, cover, and then let smoke for 45 minutes, or until internal temperature reaches 165–175 degrees. Serve with grits.

Variation: Although designed for a charcoal grill, this recipe can be prepared on a gas grill. Heat one side of the grill to medium-high and place wood chips on hot side. Then follow the directions above.

Thai Red Curry

MAKES 4 SERVINGS

4	chicken breasts
	kosher salt and pepper
2 tablespoons	olive oil
2 tablespoons	butter
2 tablespoons	vegetable oil
¾ pound	fresh French green beans
1	red bell pepper, julienned
1	yellow bell pepper, julienned
½ head	white cabbage, shredded
½ cup	fresh basil, julienned
¼ cup	ponzu sauce
	juice of 1 lime
	Red Curry Grits (see page 20)
3 pinches	fresh cilantro

Preheat oven to broil.

Sprinkle chicken with salt and pepper to taste, and then drizzle with olive oil. Cook chicken for about 45 minutes, flipping it halfway through (broil settings vary, so keep an eye on it).

Preheat a large frying pan over high heat. Add butter and vegetable oil, let foam, and then add vegetables, basil, and a pinch of salt. Mix together and let sit for about 2 minutes, stir, then let sit again. Vegetables should caramelize and release their sugars. Once vegetables have browned, reduce heat to medium-high; add ponzu and lime juice, stirring frequently for 5 minutes. Slice chicken and serve over grits, topped with vegetable mixture. Garnish with cilantro.

Black-and-Blue Grits

MAKES 4 SERVINGS

¼ cup	Worcestershire sauce
	juice of 1 lemon
	kosher salt and pepper
2 pounds	beef tenderloin, whole and trimmed
2 tablespoons	vegetable oil
8 ounces	fresh mushrooms, cleaned and sliced
1 package	phyllo sheets
2 sticks	unsalted butter, melted
	Stilton Blue Cheese Grits (see page 24)

Preheat oven to 350 degrees.

Mix Worcestershire and lemon juice together. Salt and pepper the beef, and then let marinate in liquid for 1 hour. Heat a frying pan with oil and sear beef on all sides; remove beef from pan and then add mushrooms, cooking until aromatic, about 6 minutes.

Place 1 phyllo sheet on a flat, clean surface. Using a basting brush, brush whole phyllo sheet with butter. Place another phyllo sheet on top and repeat this process with 7 sheets phyllo. Place beef in the middle on top of layered phyllo and top with mushrooms. Fold dough around beef, trimming off excess. Place on a baking sheet and bake for about 45 minutes, or until the internal temperature reaches 120–135 degrees (medium rare). Remove from oven and let rest for 10 minutes. Serve with grits.

Crab-and-Grits-Cake Burger

MAKES 6 SERVINGS

	White Stone-Ground Grits (see page 12)
1 cup	mayonnaise
	juice of 1 lemon
1 tablespoon	Old Bay Seasoning
1 dash	Worcestershire sauce
1 tablespoon	Tabasco sauce
1/3 cup	sour cream
1 pound	lump blue crabmeat
1/3 cup	Nabisco cracker meal
	zest of 2 lemons
1/3 cup	chopped jalapeños
1 cup	House-Autry Seafood Breader
1/4 cup	vegetable oil
6	hamburger buns
	toppings of choice

Prepare grits according to recipe and then chill for at least 2 hours. Add mayonnaise, lemon juice, Old Bay, Worcestershire, Tabasco, sour cream, crabmeat, lemon zest, and jalapeños, being careful not to break up crab. Form into six patties and bread with seafood breader. Pan-fry over medium-high heat with oil until crisp and golden brown on both sides, about 2–3 minutes. Serve on hamburger buns with toppings of your choice.

#54

Grilled Tuna Steaks

MAKES 4 SERVINGS

1 tablespoon	sesame oil
1 tablespoon	chili oil
1/3 cup	sake
3	scallions, cleaned and chopped
4 (6–8 ounce)	tuna steaks (sashimi grade if available)
1 jar (2 ounces)	wasabi powder
	White Stone-Ground Grits (see page 12)

In a bowl, mix together sesame and chili oils, sake, and scallions. Marinate tuna steaks in mixture at least 2 hours. Light some coals (about 1/4 of the bag) and let burn until they are very gray. Spread them evenly, scrape the grill grate, and then spray with nonstick spray oil away from the heat (spray will flame). Place grate on grill and let it get hot. (If using a gas grill, heat to medium-high.) Lightly spray tuna steaks with nonstick spray and grill for 1–2 minutes, rotate a quarter turn and then cook another minute; flip and repeat. Tuna is best served medium rare, so it should still have a warm, pink center, 130 degrees. Cooking time will be brief if done over a hot grill.

Make wasabi paste by following directions on wasabi powder jar. Stir 1 1/2 tablespoons paste into cooked grits.

Serve fish with wasabi grits.

Short Ribs with Cheddar Cheese Grits

MAKES 6 SERVINGS

5 pounds	bone-in short ribs
2 pinches	kosher salt
2 pinches	pepper
½ cup	flour
½ cup	olive oil
2	yellow onions
1 bag (12 ounces)	baby carrots
1 bag (8 ounces)	petite green beans
½ head	white cabbage
8½ cups	red wine
3 cups	beef stock
10 cloves	garlic
5	bay leaves
4 sprigs	thyme
2 stems	rosemary, leafed and finely chopped
	White Cheddar Cheese Grits (see page 23)

In a bowl, season ribs with salt and pepper and then toss with flour, mixing well. Add oil to a large Dutch oven on medium-high heat. Brown ribs evenly, 4–6 minutes. Remove ribs and cook vegetables in pan drippings for 4 minutes. Deglaze pan with half the wine, scraping down all sides and edges. Add beef stock and rest of wine. Add garlic cloves, bay leaves, thyme, and rosemary. Reduce wine and stock by one-third; add ribs back to mix and reduce heat to medium. Simmer for 1 hour, or until half the liquid has reduced. Remove bay leaves and serve grits in a bowl, topped with ribs and vegetables.

Apple-Blossom Grits and Roasted Pork Loin

MAKES 6 SERVINGS

	Yellow Stone-Ground Grits (see page 13)
1½ cups	organic apple juice
2 tablespoons	garlic powder
1 tablespoon	black pepper, plus more
1 tablespoon	dried thyme
½ tablespoon	cayenne pepper
2	pork tenderloins
3 tablespoons	vegetable oil
2	Granny Smith apples, peeled and sliced
1 large	red onion, julienned
3 tablespoons	olive oil
	kosher salt

Prepare grits according to recipe but substitute organic apple juice in place of 1½ cups water. Preheat oven to 350 degrees.

In a bowl, mix garlic powder, black pepper, thyme, and cayenne pepper for the dry rub. Rinse pork in cold water and pat dry with a paper towel. Place pork onto a platter and apply dry rub.

In a frying pan, heat vegetable oil to medium-high heat and sear pork on all sides. Toss apples and onion in a bowl with olive oil and salt and pepper to taste. Turn apple mixture out onto a roasting pan and place seared pork on top. Bake for 35–40 minutes, or until internal temperature reaches 160 degrees. Serve with grits.

Chicken Burrito with Chipotle Grits

MAKES 8 SERVINGS

	Hickory-Smoked Chicken (see page 65)
	Chipotle Grits (see page 19)
1 package	**10-inch tortillas**
4	**Roma tomatoes, chopped**
1 large	**onion, chopped**
1 jar (12–16 ounces)	**salsa**
1 can (4.5 ounces)	**chopped green chiles**
1 head	**green-leaf lettuce, cleaned and sliced into fine ribbons**
2 cups	**grated cheese**
2 cups	**guacamole**

Prepare chicken according to recipe. Once it has cooled, pick chicken apart. Build burritos in tortillas using the cooked grits and the toppings. Heat the finished burrito in the microwave for 30–45 seconds.

#58

Baked Maple Grits with Country Ham

MAKES 6 SERVINGS

	White Stone-Ground Grits (see page 12)
$\frac{1}{2}$ cup	**Vermont maple syrup**
$\frac{1}{3}$ cup	**tightly packed brown sugar**
1 pound	**high-quality country ham**

Prepare grits according to recipe and then add syrup. Preheat oven to 375 degrees.

Place grits in a 9 x 13-inch casserole dish and sprinkle with brown sugar. Bake 15–20 minutes, or until brown sugar has melted. Heat a frying pan to medium-high heat. Fry ham until brown and crispy, 8–10 minutes. Serve grits with ham.

Barbecued Shrimp and Grits Soufflé

MAKES 4–6 SERVINGS

8 cups	water
2 tablespoons	kosher salt
1	onion, roughly chopped
	juice of 1 lemon
1 pound (16–20)	shrimp, peeled and deveined
1 cup	heavy cream
1	egg
	Big R's Barbecue Grits (see page 90)

Preheat oven to 375 degrees.

In a pot, bring water, salt, onion, and lemon juice to a boil. Add shrimp and cook until just pink, about 1 minute. Remove and cool in an ice bath. Strain, roughly chop, and reserve.

In a bowl, combine cream and egg with a whisk. In a separate bowl, combine grits, cream mixture, and chopped shrimp. Transfer to an 8-inch round casserole dish, filling about three-quarters to the top. Bake 30 minutes. Serve immediately.

#60

Gouda Shrimp and Grits

MAKES 6 SERVINGS

½ pound	bacon, chopped into small pieces
1 bunch	scallions, chopped into very small rounds
1 large	sweet onion, diced
4 cloves	garlic, diced
1 pound (26–30)	shrimp, peeled and deveined
⅓ cup	Worcestershire sauce
¼ cup	white wine
	Gouda Grits (see page 22)
	Tabasco sauce
2 cups	grated Gouda cheese

Preheat oven to 350 degrees.

Cook bacon until crisp in a nonstick frying pan. Drain bacon on paper towels, reserving bacon grease in pan. Heat pan to medium-high heat, then add onions and garlic and caramelize until brown. Add shrimp and cook for 3–5 minutes. Combine Worcestershire and wine and then deglaze pan with liquid, stirring frequently. Reduce liquid by half, or until slightly thickened; remove from heat. Pour grits into a 9 x 13-inch baking dish. Pour shrimp-and-onion mixture over grits and add crumbled bacon. Use a dash of Tabasco to taste, top with cheese, and bake 15–20 minutes.

Grits and Crawfish

MAKES 6 SERVINGS

1 large	onion, diced
2	shallots, finely chopped
2 cloves	garlic, diced
$\frac{1}{2}$ pound	ground spicy sausage
$\frac{1}{2}$ cup	cooking Marsala
1$\frac{1}{2}$ pounds	crawfish tails
	Old Bay–Lemon Grits (see page 21)

Preheat oven to 325 degrees.

Heat a frying pan to medium-high heat and then add onion, shallots, and garlic and sauté until golden brown. Add sausage and cook for 7 minutes, or until cooked through. Deglaze pan with Marsala, and then add crawfish. Pour grits into a 9 x 13-inch baking dish and top with crawfish mixture. Bake for 25 minutes.

Veggie Grits Chili

MAKES 8–10 SERVINGS

1 can (8 ounces)	Rotel tomatoes, drained
2 cans (4.5 ounces each)	chopped green chiles
	White or Yellow Stone-Ground Grits (see pages 12 and 13)
1 box	vegetarian chili mix
10 cloves	garlic, minced
½ cup	sour cream
1 cup	grated cheddar cheese

Fold tomatoes and green chiles into cooked grits and cook over low heat until liquid has been absorbed. Cook veggie chili according to package directions, adding the garlic as you start cooking. When done, fold in grits. Serve with sour cream and top with cheese.

SIDE DISHES

Roasted Corn and Sun-Dried Tomatoes

MAKES 4–6 SERVINGS

1 cup	sun-dried tomatoes, julienned
2 cups	salt brine (2 cups water mixed with 2 tablespoons kosher salt)
2 cups	yellow sweet corn
¼ cup	olive oil
	salt and pepper
	White Stone-Ground Grits (see page 12)
1 package (6 ounces)	fresh goat cheese

Preheat oven to 375 degrees.

Hydrate tomatoes in the salt brine for 30 minutes. While tomatoes are hydrating, toss corn with oil and salt and pepper to taste. Drain the tomatoes and add to corn mixture. Place mixture on a rimmed baking sheet and roast for 45 minutes or until brown. Remove from oven and stir into cooked grits. Add half of the crumbled cheese to grits. Use remaining cheese for garnish once grits are plated.

Jalapeño and Bacon Grits
MAKES 4–6 SERVINGS

8 slices	thick-sliced bacon
	White or Yellow Stone-Ground Grits (see pages 12 and 13)
¼ cup	pickled jalapeño slices
	salt and pepper
	green Tabasco sauce

Slice bacon into thin strips and fry until crispy, 8–10 minutes. Drain excess bacon grease and stir fried bacon into grits. Dice jalapeño slices and add to grit mixture. Stir thoroughly and add salt and pepper to taste. Garnish with a splash of green Tabasco.

Variation: For a more spicy version, add more jalapeños. For less spicy, add fewer.

Bacon and Jalapeño Fried Grits Squares

MAKES 6–8 SERVINGS

	Instant Grits Done Right (see page 14)
8 slices	thick-sliced bacon
¼ cup	pickled jalapeño slices
	salt and pepper
1½ cups	House-Autry Seafood Breader
8 cups	peanut oil

Cook grits according to recipe. Slice bacon into thin strips and fry until crispy, 8–10 minutes. Drain excess bacon grease and add fried bacon to grits. Dice jalapeño slices and stir into grits. Pour grit mixture into a 9 x 13-inch baking dish and spread evenly. Cover tightly and refrigerate for 3–6 hours until firm. Remove from refrigerator and cut grits into half-inch squares, making 40–45 squares. Place seafood breader in a deep bowl. Carefully bread 5–6 squares at a time.

Preheat oil to 375 degrees in a deep fryer or on the stovetop in a fry-safe pot. Add 10–12 breaded grit squares to preheated oil. Fry until golden brown, 4–6 minutes. Serve as an accompaniment to any low-country dish.

Parmesan-Encrusted Grits Croutons

MAKES 6–8 SERVINGS

	Roasted Garlic–Infused Grits (see page 18)
1 cup	grated Parmesan cheese, divided
1 tablespoon	Italian seasoning
1 cup	House-Autry Seafood Breader
8 cups	peanut oil

Prepare grits according to recipe. Stir ½ cup Parmesan into grits. Spread grit mixture evenly onto a half-size sheet pan. Cover and refrigerate for 3–6 hours until firm. Toss the remaining ½ cup cheese, Italian seasoning, and seafood breader together in a bowl. Once grits are firm, cut into small crouton-size pieces and carefully coat with dry-ingredient mixture.

Preheat oil to 375 degrees in a deep fryer or on stovetop in a fry-safe pot. Add 10–12 croutons to preheated oil. Fry until golden brown and crispy, 5–7 minutes. Great with Caesar salads.

Roasted Jalapeño-and-Cherry Stuffing

MAKES 6–8 SERVINGS

	Yellow Stone-Ground Grits (see page 13)
5	fresh whole jalapeños
1 cup	dried cherries
¼ cup	olive oil
	salt and pepper
1 cup	uncooked stovetop stuffing
4 sprigs	fresh rosemary, chopped
½ stick	lightly salted butter, melted
1	egg
½ cup	milk

Prepare grits according to recipe. Preheat oven to 350 degrees.

Cut off tops of jalapeños. Slice in half, core, and remove seeds. Toss jalapeños and cherries in olive oil with a scant pinch of salt and pepper. In a roasting pan, roast mixture in oven for 30–45 minutes. Remove from oven and transfer mixture to cutting board, coarsely chop cherries and peppers, and set aside.

Place stuffing in a mixing bowl with rosemary, melted butter, egg, and milk. Add jalapeños and cherries. Beat with fork. Fold in the stuffing, then add grits in four additions, mixing thoroughly each time. Place in a 9 x 13-inch greased casserole dish, and bake for 45–50 minutes, or until golden brown on top. Stuffing is especially good with pork tenderloin and collard greens.

Stuffed Bell Peppers

MAKES 6 SERVINGS

1 small	sweet onion, diced
2 tablespoons	vegetable oil, divided
½ pound	ground sirloin
1 teaspoon	garlic powder
1 teaspoon	onion powder
	salt and pepper
1 can (8 ounces)	Rotel tomatoes, with liquid
	White Stone-Ground Grits (see page 12)
6 large	bell peppers, topped, cored, and seeded
1 cup	grated cheddar cheese

Preheat oven to 375 degrees.

Brown onion in 1 tablespoon oil in a large pan. Add sirloin, garlic powder, onion powder, and salt and pepper, to taste. Cook meat through, 10–12 minutes, then add tomatoes with liquid. Cook until liquid is reduced by half; remove from stove and fold in grits.

Coat the inside and outside of bell peppers with remaining oil, plus more salt and pepper to taste. Stuff peppers with grit mixture and place on baking sheet. Bake for 20–30 minutes. For the last 5 minutes, top with cheddar cheese and cook until melted.

Scallion Cheesy Biscuits

MAKES 6–8 SERVINGS

1 bunch	scallions, finely chopped
³⁄₄ cup	dry instant grits
5 tablespoons	butter, at room temperature, divided
2 tablespoons	brown sugar
4 tablespoons	baking powder
1¹⁄₄ cups	flour
1 cup	grated sharp Vermont white cheddar cheese
¹⁄₂ cup	milk

Preheat oven to 425 degrees.

Brown onions in a frying pan with 1 tablespoon of butter for 7 minutes over medium-high heat, stirring frequently. In a bowl, combine grits, brown sugar, baking powder, and flour. Cut in remaining 4 tablespoons butter with a fork until mixture resembles coarse crumbs. Add cheese, scallions, and milk. Mix until dry ingredients are moist and then knead four or five times on a floured surface. Roll out into 9-inch circles and then cut with a medium biscuit cutter or rim of a drinking glass. Place on a parchment-lined baking sheet, and cook 20–25 minutes, or until golden brown.

Cheese Bread

MAKES 6–8 SERVINGS

3 cups	bread flour, divided
1 cup	uncooked instant grits
¼ cup	powdered milk
1 tablespoon	yeast
1 teaspoon	kosher salt
1	egg
½ cup	vegetable oil
2 cups	warm water
1 cup	grated pepper jack cheese
2 tablespoons	butter, melted

Preheat oven to 350 degrees.

In a bowl, mix 2 cups of flour with grits, milk, yeast, and salt. In a separate bowl, combine egg, oil, and water. Stir into flour mixture until well blended. Add cheese and remaining 1 cup flour as needed until dough comes together. Knead two to four times on a floured surface. Place dough in a bowl, cover, and let rise about 30 minutes, until double in size. Punch down dough and place into a loaf pan; let rise again until double in size. Lightly brush top with melted butter and bake 30–45 minutes until golden brown.

Ma Ethel's Mixed Bread

MAKES 6–8 SERVINGS

1 envelope	yeast
2 cups	warm water
2 tablespoons	vegetable shortening
2 tablespoons	sugar
2 teaspoons	salt
2 cups	White or Yellow Stone-Ground Grits (see pages 12 and 13)
4 cups	flour

In a bowl, dissolve yeast in warm water. Add shortening, sugar, salt, and cooked grits. Stir in enough flour to make a stiff batter. Cover and let rise until double in size, about 30 minutes. Knead with hands and divide into two well-greased loaf pans. Let rise until double in size, about 30 minutes. When ready to bake, preheat oven to 400 degrees and bake about 50 minutes until golden brown.

Grits and Black Beans

MAKES 6 SERVINGS

2 cans (15 ounces each)	**black beans**
2 teaspoons	**cumin**
dash	**cayenne pepper**
1 tablespoon	**granulated sugar**
	juice of 1 lime
	White Stone-Ground Grits (see page 12)
	cilantro

Drain and rinse 1 can beans. Place beans in a nonstick pot and add the other can with the liquid. Add cumin, cayenne pepper, sugar, and lime juice. Cook over medium heat until beans thicken, about 20 minutes. Spoon over grits and garnish with cilantro.

Big R's Barbecue Grits

MAKES 4–6 SERVINGS

Big R's Barbecue Sauce*:

2 cups	ketchup
1 cup	apple cider vinegar
1 cup	water
1 teaspoon	kosher salt
1 teaspoon	black pepper
1 teaspoon	cayenne pepper
2 teaspoons	chili powder
1/8 cup	brown sugar

White Stone-Ground Grits (see page 12) or instant grits

In a pot, simmer all sauce ingredients over low heat for 1 hour, stirring frequently. Fold barbecue sauce into cooked grits and enjoy.

*Recipe courtesy of Randolph "Big R" Stafford.

Vidalia Onion Casserole
MAKES 6 SERVINGS

4 tablespoons	**vegetable oil**
3	**large Vidalia onions, julienned**
2	**eggs**
½ cup	**chopped pickled jalapeños**
	White Stone-Ground Grits (see page 12)
1½ cups	**sharp cheddar cheese**

Preheat oven to 350 degrees.

Heat a frying pan over high heat and add oil and onions; cook until onions are caramelized, 8–10 minutes.

In a bowl, beat eggs and fold in onions and jalapeños. Add this mixture to cooked grits. Pour grits into a 9 x 13-inch baking dish and top with cheese. Bake for 35–40 minutes. Remove and serve.

Very Garlicky Grits Casserole
MAKES 6–8 SERVINGS

1 stick	unsalted butter, softened (reserve 2 tablespoons for buttering baking dish)
2	eggs, beaten well
1 tube	garlic cheese
½ cup	half-and-half
	White Stone-Ground Grits (see page 12)
½ cup	Nabisco cracker meal
½ cup	crumbled corn flakes

Preheat oven to 350 degrees.

In a bowl, mix together butter, eggs, cheese, and half-and-half. Fold into grits in three additions. Pour grits into a buttered 2-quart baking dish.

In a small bowl, mix together cracker meal and corn flakes. Top grits with this mixture. Bake for 20–30 minutes, or until top has browned nicely.

#76
Panhandle Grits
MAKES 8–10 SERVINGS

1 pound	thick-cut bacon
2 medium	onions, finely chopped
1	green bell pepper, diced
1	red bell pepper, diced
1½ cups	finely chopped country ham
2 cans (15 ounces each)	Rotel tomatoes, drained
	White Stone-Ground Grits (see page 12)

In a frying pan, fry bacon and set aside. Sauté onions and bell peppers in 2–3 tablespoons bacon drippings until browned. Add ham and stir well. Sauté over medium-low heat for 15 minutes. Add tomatoes and simmer for 30 minutes. When grits are cooked, add ham mixture and stir well. Serve hot with bacon crumbled on top.

Recipe concept from Coffee Cup Restaurant, Pensacola, Florida.

Extra Cheese Grits Soufflé

MAKES 8–10 SERVINGS

½ cup	grated extra sharp cheddar cheese
½ cup	grated extra sharp white cheddar cheese
1 cup	melted butter
4	eggs, well beaten
½ cup	milk
	kosher salt and pepper
	White Stone-Ground Grits (see page 12)

Preheat oven to 350 degrees.

Stir cheeses, butter, eggs, milk, and salt and pepper to taste into grits. Stir until cheese is melted and milk has been absorbed, about 20 minutes. Pour into a buttered 3-quart baking dish and bake for 1 hour.

Baked Gruyère Grits Casserole

MAKES 4 SERVINGS

	White Stone-Ground Grits (see page 12)
1 can (8 ounces)	**Rotel tomatoes, Italian blend, drained**
1½ cups	**grated Gruyère cheese**

Preheat oven to 350 degrees.

Pour grits into a 9 x 13-inch greased baking dish and then top with tomatoes and cheese. Bake for 25 minutes, or until cheese has browned nicely.

#79-97

DESSERTS

Caramel Grits

MAKES 4 SERVINGS

	Sweet Vanilla Grits (see page 26)
1 jar (12.25 ounces)	caramel sauce
1 pint	ice cream, any flavor
1 cup	chopped pecans, toasted

Prepare grits according to recipe. Add caramel and mix well. Serve grits spooned over ice cream and topped with chopped pecans.

Seasonal Berry Crepe

MAKES 6–8 SERVINGS

	sweet grits recipe of choice (see pages 26–31)
1 package	fresh crepes
	fresh berries

Prepare grits according to recipe. Fill crepes with grits and berries; roll up and top with more berries. Serve hot or at room temperature.

Southern Chocolate Grits Truffles

MAKES 75 INDIVIDUAL TRUFFLES

Chocolate Grits (see page 27)
2 pounds **high-quality baker's milk chocolate, divided**

Prepare grits according to recipe. Chill for 2–4 hours or until set firm. Roll grits into ½-inch balls. Place onto two parchment-lined sheet pans and refrigerate.

In a pot, heat ¼ inch water to boil. Chop chocolate into small pieces and place 1 pound chocolate in a glass bowl. Place glass bowl over boiling water to create a double boiler. Melt chocolate until smooth. Remove one sheet pan from refrigerator. Submerge each truffle one at a time in melted chocolate, removing with fork and placing back on parchment. Repeat until all truffles are coated, melting remaining 1 pound chocolate as needed with double-boiler method. Let truffles rest for 20 minutes before serving.

Variation: Substitute white chocolate for milk chocolate.

Vanilla Bean Brûlée

MAKES 6 SERVINGS

	Sweet Vanilla Grits (see page 26)
2 cups	**granulated sugar**
	berries

Prepare grits according to recipe. Fill six ramekins evenly with grits and chill 2 hours. Moisten ramekin tops with wet paper towel. Place sugar in a bowl. Spoon sugar over top of ramekin, coating the top of the grits evenly. Remove any excess sugar by flipping ramekin upside down in bowl. If not coated evenly, repeat. Caramelize sugar with a brûlée torch and serve with fresh garden berries of your choice.

For a smoother texture, use instant grits.

White Chocolate Brûlée

MAKES 6 SERVINGS

	Sweet Vanilla Grits (see page 26)
1 bag (11 ounces)	**Ghirardelli white-chocolate chips**
2 cups	**granulated sugar**
	berries

Prepare grits according to recipe. When finished, fold in white-chocolate chips. Fill six ramekins evenly and chill 3 hours. Moisten tops of ramekins with wet paper towel. Place sugar in a bowl. Spoon sugar over top of each ramekin, coating the tops of grits evenly. Remove any excess sugar by flipping ramekin upside down in bowl. If not coated evenly, repeat. Caramelize sugar with a brûlée torch and serve with fresh garden berries of your choice.

#84
Espresso Grits Brûlée
MAKES 6 SERVINGS

Espresso Grits (see page 24)
2 cups **granulated sugar**
berries

Prepare grits according to recipe. Fill six ramekins evenly with grits and chill 2–3 hours. Moisten tops with wet paper towel. Place sugar in a large bowl. Spoon sugar over top of ramekins, coating top of grits evenly. Remove any excess sugar by flipping ramekin upside down in bowl. If not coated evenly, repeat. Caramelize sugar with a brûlée torch and serve with fresh garden berries of your choice.

For a smoother texture, use instant grits.

Fried Chocolate Grits

MAKES 6–8 SERVINGS

	Chocolate Grits (see page 27)
2 cups	flour
1 tablespoon	cornstarch
1 teaspoon	salt
1	cup sugar
5 cups	vegetable oil
	ice cream

Prepare grits according to recipe. Pour into a 9 x 13-inch dish. Cool 2–3 hours. Cut grits into bite-size pieces or use cookie cutters to make varying shapes. Make any shape you want, but they should not be more than a bite or so.

In a bowl, mix together all dry ingredients. In a frying pan, heat oil. Bread grits in dry-ingredient mixture and fry over medium-high heat until golden brown, 6–8 minutes. Serve over your favorite ice cream.

Orange and Maple Cream Pudding

MAKES 10–12 SERVINGS

½ cup	light brown sugar
4 large	eggs
	zest of 2 oranges
⅓ cup	fresh orange juice
4 tablespoons	unsalted butter, divided
1 tablespoon	dark corn syrup
1 tablespoon	pure maple syrup
1 tablespoon	dark rum
½ teaspoon	salt
½ teaspoon	cinnamon
½ teaspoon	ground ginger
½ teaspoon	ground cloves
	Sweet Vanilla Grits (see page 26)
½ cup	chopped pecans
¼ cup	dark brown sugar
	vanilla ice cream

Preheat oven to 350 degrees.

In a bowl, mix together light brown sugar, eggs, orange zest and juice, 2 tablespoons butter, corn and maple syrups, rum, salt, cinnamon, ginger, and cloves, with an electric mixer until smooth. Add grits and mix to incorporate until well blended.

In a separate bowl, mix pecans, dark brown sugar, and remaining 2 tablespoons unsalted butter and then set aside. Pour grit mixture into a buttered 9 x 13-inch baking dish and bake 25 minutes. Remove and top with pecan mixture; bake another 20 minutes, or until top is caramelized. Serve hot with ice cream.

Chocolate Grits and Sweet Waffles

MAKES 8 SERVINGS

	Chocolate Grits (see page 27)
2	eggs
2 cups	milk
5 tablespoons	vegetable oil
3 cups	flour
3 teaspoons	baking powder
1 teaspoon	kosher salt
2 teaspoons	sugar
1 teaspoon	baking soda
1 cup	water
1 pint	pistachio ice cream

Prepare grits according to recipe and keep over low heat while preparing waffles.

In a bowl, beat eggs, milk, and oil together. In a separate bowl, mix flour, baking powder, salt, and sugar and then add egg mixture. Dissolve baking soda in water and add to batter; batter will be thin. You can keep the batter in the refrigerator for a few days. When you want to use it, just add a little extra baking powder and you're good to go. Fill waffle iron with batter and cook until golden brown, 6–8 minutes.

Place two sections of a waffle on a plate and top each with grits. Top with 1–2 scoops ice cream.

Strawberry Grits with Balsamic Reduction

MAKES 6 SERVINGS

1 pint	balsamic vinegar
½ cup	sugar
	Strawberry Grits (see page 30)
2 cups	sliced fresh strawberries

In a 4-quart pot, bring vinegar and sugar to a boil and reduce heat to medium high. Simmer until it has reduced by three-fourths and has become a syrup. Serve grits topped with fresh berries and balsamic reduction.

#89
Grits Neapolitan

MAKES 10–12 SERVINGS

½ batch **Sweet Vanilla Grits (see page 26)**
½ batch **Strawberry Grits (see page 30)**
½ batch **Chocolate Grits (see page 27)**

Prepare grits according to recipes. Line a loaf pan with plastic wrap and layer vanilla grits, strawberry grits, and chocolate grits. Let cool. Serve chilled or frozen.

Hazelnut Trifle

MAKES 6 SERVINGS

2 packages (3 ounces each)	**ladyfingers, quartered**
1 cup	**raspberry liqueur**
½ cup	**cocoa powder, for garnish**
	Hazelnut Grits (see page 29)
2 cups	**whipped cream**
1 pint	**fresh raspberries**
	mint sprigs

Soak ladyfingers in raspberry liqueur. Rim six deep martini glasses with extra liqueur and coat with cocoa. Place some ladyfingers in the bottom of the glasses, then top with grits and then whipped cream. Repeat layering until glasses are full. Chill for at least 3 hours. Garnish with fresh raspberries and mint sprigs to serve.

Key Lime Trifle
MAKES 6 SERVINGS

	zest of 2 Key limes
	Key Lime Grits (see page 31)
	juice of 1 Key lime
2 cups	crushed graham crackers
2 cups	whipped cream
6	Key lime slices

Fold lime zest into cooked grits. Rim six deep martini glasses with some key lime juice and coat with some cracker crumbs. Place some cracker crumbs in the bottom of each glass, top with a small amount of grits and whipped cream, and repeat until filled. Chill for at least 3 hours, and garnish with lime slices to serve.

Hazelnut Grits Napoleon

MAKES 6 SERVINGS

½ cup	hazelnuts
1 package	Pillsbury Puff Pastry Dough
1	egg
2 tablespoons	milk
	Hazelnut Grits (see page 29)
1½ cups	fresh assorted berries, sliced
1 cup	whipped cream

Toast hazelnuts for about 6 minutes or until they become aromatic, then place them in middle of a kitchen towel. Rub them together aggressively to remove the skin. In a food processor or on a cutting board, coarsely chop hazelnuts; set aside. Place puff pastry on a sheet pan lined with parchment paper.

In a bowl, mix egg and milk well. Brush a small amount egg mixture over dough and bake according to package directions. Cut pastry into six pieces and divide each piece into three by pulling apart from the top. Place one piece of pastry on a plate, and top with grits, berries, and nuts. Place another piece of pastry on top and repeat layering. Place the third piece of pastry on top and add a dollop of whipped cream, berries, and nuts.

Tiramisu

MAKES 6 SERVINGS

6	egg yolks
1 cup	sugar
¾ cup	Sweet Vanilla Grits (see page 26)
1 cup	mascarpone cheese
3	egg whites
½ cup	cold espresso
¼ cup	rum
2 packages (3 ounces each)	ladyfingers
	cocoa powder

In a bowl, combine egg yolks and sugar, beating until light and creamy with an electric mixer. In a separate bowl, fold grits into cheese in two additions. Add grit mixture to egg mixture 3 tablespoons at a time until smooth and creamy.

In a third bowl, beat egg whites until stiff peaks form. (Be careful not to use a bowl with any oil residue because the egg whites will not stiffen.) Fold in the grit mixture in three or four additions.

In a small bowl, mix espresso and rum. Separate the ladyfingers and place them in a 9-inch-square baking pan. Evenly soak ladyfingers with half the espresso mixture and then top with grit mixture and repeat. Dust top with cocoa powder and chill at least 3 hours.

Rum Raisin and Banana Porridge

MAKES 4–6 SERVINGS

½ stick	unsalted butter
1 cup	golden raisins
⅓ cup	dark rum
½ cup	packed brown sugar
2 ripe	bananas, sliced in small pieces
	Sweet Vanilla Grits (see page 26)

Heat frying pan over medium-high heat, add butter, and let foam dissipate. Add raisins and cook for 3 minutes. Add rum and then reduce by half; add sugar. Let sugar melt and add bananas. Cook for 2 minutes in sugar and remove from heat. Top grits with rum-raisin mixture.

Strawberry Shortcakes

MAKES 8 SERVINGS

2½ cups	chopped fresh strawberries
1 cup	sugar
1	angel food cake
2 cups	whipped cream
	Strawberry Grits (see page 30)
	mint sprigs

In a bowl, combine strawberries and sugar and refrigerate
for 2 hours to form strawberry liquor. Slice angel food cake in
four uniform slices across the top to make layers. Spread some
whipped cream across the bottom and top with grits and
strawberries, drizzling some of the juices on top. Repeat; once
all four layers are finished, top cake with the remaining berries
and cream. Garnish each serving with mint.

Chocolate–Cream Cheese Cake

MAKES 9 SERVINGS

1 box	chocolate cake mix
4	eggs
$^1/_2$ cup	melted butter
1 cup	uncooked instant grits
$1^1/_2$ cups	powdered sugar
1 package (8 ounces)	cream cheese
1 teaspoon	vanilla
$^1/_3$ cup	flour
1 pint	vanilla ice cream
1 pint	fresh raspberries

Preheat oven to 350 degrees.

In a bowl, mix cake mix, 2 eggs, butter, and grits.

In a separate bowl, use an electric mixer to beat together remaining 2 eggs, powdered sugar, cream cheese, and vanilla until smooth. Grease a 9 x 13-inch cake pan and sprinkle with flour to coat the pan; discard extra flour. Spread the cake mix in the pan and top with the cream cheese mixture. Bake 45 minutes, or until a toothpick is inserted and comes out clean. Top with ice cream and raspberries.

Grits with Tart Granny Smith Apples

MAKES 6 SERVINGS

1 cup	heavy cream
2 cups	milk
2 teaspoons	ground cinnamon
½ teaspoon	vanilla
½ cup	granulated sugar
¾ cups	uncooked instant grits
1 teaspoon	salt
3	Granny Smith apples
⅓ cup	packed brown sugar
3 tablespoons	unsalted butter
1 jar (12.25 ounces)	caramel sauce

Heat a nonstick pot to medium-low heat. Add cream, milk, cinnamon, vanilla, and sugar. Bring to boil and add grits and salt. Cook on low heat for 35–40 minutes, or until grits have absorbed the liquid. Stir grits occasionally. Grease six 1-cup ramekins. Spoon grits into ramekins and refrigerate overnight.

Before serving, peel apples and slice into thin slivers. In a bowl, mix together apples and brown sugar. Heat a large frying pan to medium-high, add butter, and cook apples until sugar has melted and apples have browned. Heat caramel sauce in microwave, place ramekins in the microwave, and heat for no more than 20 seconds; grits may fall because of cream. Serve grits with caramel and apples.

HOMINY GRITS

Boiled Hominy

MAKES 4–6 SERVINGS

1 can (15.5 ounces)	**white hominy**
3 cups	**chicken stock**
⅓ cup	**distilled vinegar**
	kosher salt

In a pot, combine hominy, stock, vinegar, and salt to taste. Boil for 1 hour or more, stirring frequently to avoid lumps.

Adapted from The Savannah Cook Book, *by Harriet Ross Colquitt, 1933.*

Fried Hominy
MAKES 4–6 SERVINGS

2 cans (15.5 ounces each)	white hominy
2	eggs
1 log (8 ounces)	goat cheese
	kosher salt and pepper
1 cup	Nabisco cracker meal
¼ cup	oil, or as needed

On a platter, spread out the hominy about 1 inch thick to get it cold. Slice this cold mixture into any shape desired. In a bowl, beat eggs and cheese together; add salt and pepper to taste. Roll mixture first in eggs, then in cracker meal to coat. Heat oil in a frying pan over medium-high heat and fry hominy for 10–12 minutes until golden brown.

Adapted from The Savannah Cook Book, *by Harriet Ross Colquitt, 1933.*

#100
Hominy Casserole
MAKES 4–6 SERVINGS

2 cups	cold hominy
1½ cups	grated white cheddar cheese
2 bunches	scallions, chopped
2	eggs, well beaten
1 tablespoon	butter
2 cups	milk
	kosher salt

Preheat oven to 350 degrees. Mash cold hominy well to remove the lumps. Fold in 1 cup cheese and scallions. Add eggs, butter, milk, and salt to taste. Put in a buttered 9 x 13-inch baking dish, top with remaining ½ cup cheese, and bake for 40 minutes.

Adapted from The Savannah Cook Book, *by Harriet Ross Colquitt, 1933.*

Southwest Baked Hominy

MAKES 6 SERVINGS

2 cans (15.5 ounces each)	white hominy
1 large	sweet onion, chopped
2 cups	sour cream
1½ cups	grated pepper jack cheese
1 can (4.5 ounces)	chopped green chiles
2	eggs
	kosher salt
4 tablespoons	butter, divided
1 cup	Nabisco cracker meal

Preheat oven to 350 degrees. In a bowl, mix hominy, onion, sour cream, cheese, chiles, eggs, and salt to taste. Grease a 9 x 13-inch baking dish with 2 tablespoons butter and add mixture. Top with cracker meal. Cut remaining 2 tablespoons butter into small pieces and spread across the top. Bake for 35 minutes or until browned on top.

NOTES

NOTES

NOTES

NOTES

NOTES

Metric Conversion Chart

VOLUME MEASUREMENTS		WEIGHT MEASUREMENTS		TEMPERATURE CONVERSION	
U.S.	Metric	U.S.	Metric	Fahrenheit	Celsius
1 teaspoon	5 ml	1/2 ounce	15 g	250	120
1 tablespoon	15 ml	1 ounce	30 g	300	150
1/4 cup	60 ml	3 ounces	90 g	325	160
1/3 cup	75 ml	4 ounces	115 g	350	180
1/2 cup	125 ml	8 ounces	225 g	375	190
2/3 cup	150 ml	12 ounces	350 g	400	200
3/4 cup	175 ml	1 pound	450 g	425	220
1 cup	250 ml	2 1/4 pounds	1 kg	450	230

MORE 101 THINGS® IN THESE

FAVORITES

AIR FRYER	**INSTANT POT**®
BACON	**PICKLE**
BUNDT® **PAN**	**RAMEN NOODLES**
CAKE MIX	**SLOW COOKER**
CASSEROLE	**TORTILLA**

Each 128 pages, $12.99

About the Author

A true southerner living in Greenville, South Carolina, **Harriss Cottingham** knows grits. His passion for food began as a young boy while taste-testing for his grandfather, who was an amateur chef.

Cottingham learned the culinary arts at Johnson and Wales University Culinary School in Charleston, South Carolina, and has worked in several fine-dining restaurants. Now a sales representative for a wine distributor, he owns and operates Catering by Harriss, featuring cooking classes and small-group events.